LAURA OWEN & KOR

Winnie AND Wilbur

Mini
WINNIE

OXFORD
UNIVERSITY PRESS

CONTENTS

WINNIE'S
Awful Auntie

WINNIE
Goes Cleaning

WINNIE
and the
Ghost in the Post

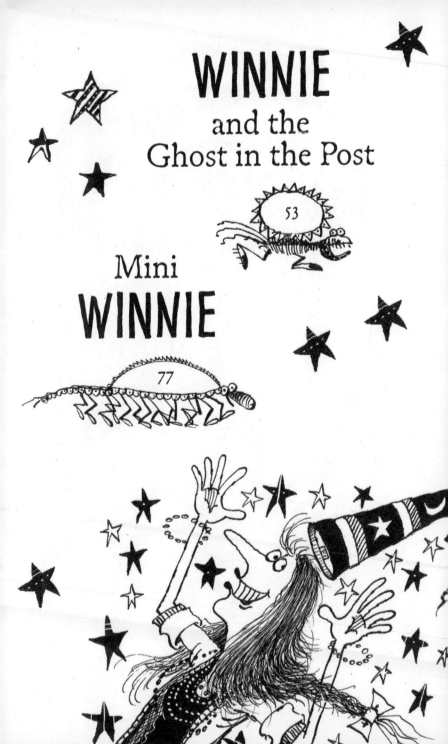

53

Mini
WINNIE

77

WINNIE'S
Awful Auntie

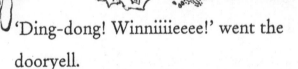

'Ding-dong! Winniiiieeee!' went the
dooryell.

'What? Who? Where am I?' Winnie sat
up in bed, suddenly awake. 'Did you hear
something, Wilbur?'

Wilbur rolled over, stretched, yawned,
and flopped back into sleep.

'Just a dream then,' said Winnie. She lay
down, stretched, yawned and . . .

'Wiiiinnnniiiiieeee!' went the dooryell.

'Oh, nits' knickers, there really is somebody there,' muttered Winnie. 'I'd better have a look.'

Winnie went to the window and peeped out. 'Oh, gnats' kneecaps, it's Auntie Aggie. Look at all that luggage! She's planning to stay!'

Wilbur buried his head under the sheets.

'It's no good hiding,' said Winnie. 'She always knows.' Winnie called out of the window, 'I'll be down in the shake of a maggot's bottom, Auntie Aggie.'

Winnie picked up her wand. 'I'd better make the place smell right for aunties. Brace yourself, Wilbur. *Abracadabra!*'

And instantly the lovely comfortable smell of mildew and mould was replaced by the sweety-tweety-neaty smell of pink petally rosy-posy pong.

'Mrrow!' complained Wilbur, putting a paw to his nose.

'I know!' said Winnie. 'Here, have a clothes peg.'

'Winifred Isaspell Tabitha Charmaine Hortense, will you please open this pesky door?!' Auntie Aggie's voice made Winnie's house shake.

'Deep breath, Wilbur. I'm going to let her in.'

Auntie Aggie seemed to fill the house with pinkness. She looked at Winnie, pointed at the clothes peg on her nose, and said, 'What in the witchy world is *that* for?'

'Oh, didn't you dow dat dese are da noo fashion?' said Winnie.

'How silly you young people are!' said Auntie Aggie. 'Take it off at once!'

11

'Yes, Auntie Aggie,' said Winnie.

Auntie Aggie pulled a hanky from her sleeve, spat on it, then wiped it over Winnie's face.

'Yeuch, get off!' said Winnie.

'I've come to sort you out, young lady,' said Auntie Aggie.

'But I don't—' began Winnie.

'Don't argue!' said Auntie Aggie. 'Now, where to begin?' She looked around the kitchen and tutted. 'Dear, oh dear!' She bent over, sticking her large pink-frocked bottom in the air, as she took rubber gloves from her bag, and pulled them on.

Then she waved her wipe-clean between-every-wish wand. 'Spit spot!' she commanded, and instantly all Winnie's stuff leapt up onto shelves and into cupboards.

S*lam***-***s***lam***-***s***lam** went the cupboard doors.

'Now I won't know where anything *is!*' wailed Winnie.

'Nonsense!' said Auntie Aggie. 'I'll smarten you up next.'

'But I don't—' began Winnie.

'Spit spot!' went Auntie Aggie, and instantly Winnie was swallowed in a smart business suit and her hair neatly styled.

Wilbur was tittering into his paws. 'Me-he-he-ow!'

14

Auntie Aggie looked at Wilbur. 'That
stinky cat has got to be changed!' she said,
and she raised her wipe-clean-between-
every-wish wand and—

'No!' said Winnie. She leapt towards
Wilbur, but her suit skirt was tight and
her legs went **wang!** and she fell **bang!**
onto the floor.

Suddenly Wilbur wasn't a cat any more.

'What have you done, you silly old sponge pudding?' wailed Winnie. 'Where's my Wilbur?'

'He's become a sweet little clean little wabbit,' said Auntie Aggie.

'But I want *Wilbur!*' wailed Winnie. 'My *Wilbur!* I'm a witch, not a magician! Give Wilbur back!'

'Er . . . no,' said Auntie Aggie. 'You young people don't know what's best. You'll soon love Wilbur the wabbit more than you ever loved that stinky cat. He can live in a nice pink cage.'

'Never!' said Winnie. She was gazing into the wabbit's eyes. She could see real Wilbur trapped inside the silly face with floppy ears.

Auntie Aggie wagged a plump finger at her. 'You wait, Winifred. When I'm an old witch I won't have the energy or magic to help you like this, and then you'll be sorry!'

Twitter-twee twitter-twee.

'It's my phone,' said Auntie Aggie. 'I'll take it outside and be back in a jiffy.'

Out bustled Auntie Aggie.

'Don't panic, Wilbur!' said Winnie. 'I'll have you out of there in one snail-second, but first I'm going to magic Auntie Aggie!'

'Snuffle?' asked Wilbur.

'Yes,' said Winnie. 'Did you hear Auntie Aggie say that she'd not be able to do magic on us once she's an old lady? So I'm going to turn her into an old lady, just for as long as she stays here. Then I'll get you back, my Wilbur, my friend, my companion cat!'

As Auntie Aggie came back into the room, reaching for her wipe-clean-between-every-wish wand, Winnie waved her own wand. She shut her eyes tight and wished with all her might, 'Make Auntie Aggie much much older than me—*Abracadabra!*'

Gasp! went Auntie Aggie.

Gasp-nibble! went Wilbur the wabbit.

'Waaaaaaa!' went a little Winnie baby on the floor.

Wilbur glared at Winnie's wand, but

there was nothing wrong with the wand's magic. Auntie Aggie *was* much much older than Winnie, because Winnie had gone backwards and become her baby self!

'Is that you, Winnie?' said Auntie Aggie.

She moved towards the door. 'Oo, I can't abide babies! Noisy smelly nasty things! I had to wait so many many years until you were old enough for me to work on you, Winnie, and now look what you've done!'

'Waaaaa!' went baby Winnie, kicking her legs and waving her fists. Then suddenly baby Winnie went quiet. A look of concentration came over her face. And a stinky smell filled the room.

'**Poooooey!** Ooo, dear!' said Auntie
Aggie. 'Quick, where's that clothes peg?
That's it, I'm off!' And off she went,
grabbing her bags and hurrying out of
Winnie's house and away.

Meanwhile, baby Winnie had got on to her hands and knees and was crawling at top speed out of the door.

Snuffle-nibble! went Wilbur the wabbit, but baby Winnie took no notice. So Wilbur the wabbit struggled with silly paws to pick up Winnie's wand.

24

Then he hopped the wand all over the lawn—boing! boing!—hopping in the shape of an '*A*' and—boing! boing!—in the shape of a '*C*' and then an '*r*' ... until he'd spelled out the whole of *Abracadabra!*

Then, instantly, Winnie was back to her old self.

'Wilbur, you're a genius!' she said. Then she waved the wand. '*Abracadabra!*'

And instantly Wilbur was back to being proper Wilbur the cat again.

'Meow!' said Wilbur. 'Meow meow meow!'

'I know,' said Winnie. 'I'll be more careful what I wish for next time! But I don't think we'll see Auntie Aggie for a while!' Winnie patted Wilbur's tatty head. 'Oo, Wilbur, I'm so very very glad you're not really a wabbit!'

WINNIE

Goes Cleaning

''Tishoo!' *Sniff-sniff*, went Wilbur.

'Use that bat as a hanky,' said Winnie.
'What d'you want for lunch?'

Wilbur opened his mouth, but no
sound came out.

'You've lost your voice!' said Winnie.
'I know a cure for that!' Winnie opened
cupboards. She grabbed this and that and
a few of those.

Chop, slice, grate, bash, squeeze, slurp-slop, ready for the oven.

'Out of the way, Wilbur! I need a rack to stretch it on.'

But Wilbur didn't move fast enough. His tail was caught in the cupboard door.

Wilbur's fur stood on end, and he yelled a silent big **yeeeooowwl!**

30

He hit the ceiling then crashed to the floor. His tail was bent and there was a large lump on his head. Wilbur's mouth opened in a pitiful silent meow.

'Blooming heck!' said Winnie. She
wiped sticky hands down her front and
went to fetch her first aid box.

'Nice fresh leeches?' she said, but
Wilbur shook his head hard. 'Just crushed
earwigs for the headache and a bandage,
then,' said Winnie.

32

Winnie found something to use as a
splint. She wound sticky plaster round
Wilbur's tail to hold the splint in place.

'There!' she said. 'I'm good at this,
aren't I? I should have been a doctor
instead of a witch!'

Later, down in the village, Winnie noticed something outside the school.

'Cleaning Operative urgently required for village school'

'Ooo, look, Wilbur!' said Winnie. 'It says . . .' Winnie ran a finger slowly along the word beginning with 'O'. '"O." "P." "E." "R . . ."' It says "operations", doesn't it? Ooo, Wilbur, they want somebody to do operations! Here's my chance to be a doctor!'

G
TIVE
uired
eschool

Wilbur put out a paw to try and grab
hold of Winnie's cardigan, but Winnie was
already at the door, pushing a button and
talking to the wall.

35

'You again!' said Mrs Parmar, the school secretary, when she opened the door. 'I remember you from when you cooked our school dinner. Out!'

'But I've come for the job,' said Winnie.

Mrs Parmar sagged. 'Well,' she sighed. 'I am desperate.'

'Where does it hurt?' asked Winnie.

'Don't touch me!' said Mrs Parmar. 'Just follow me.'

Mrs Parmar gave Winnie a pinny to wear.

'Here's your equipment,' she said, opening a cupboard.

'Really?' said Winnie. 'I can understand the bucket, but when does a doctor need spray polish?'

'Doctor?' boomed Mrs Parmar. 'The job is for a *cleaner*!'

'You want to waste my skills on dusting?' said Winnie.

'Oh, please do it, Winnie!' said Mrs Parmar, suddenly wilting. 'It's Parents' Evening tonight. If the school isn't clean they'll all take their children away and the school will close and I'll be out of a job and I'll have no money and I'll have to live in a cardboard box and I'll starve so thin I'll slip down the drain grating and then the sewer rats will get me and they'll nibble me and I don't like being nibbled and . . .'

'I don't like being nibbled myself, Mrs Parmar,' said Winnie. 'I'll do it.'

'Marvellous!' said Mrs Parmar. 'Everywhere must be clean by the end-of-school time.'

'Easy-peasy lemon squeezy!' said Winnie.

'I don't think much of this kind of broom,' said Winnie. 'Where's my proper broom, Wilbur?'

Winnie's broom swept double-quick. It brushed floors and walls and ceilings. It even tried to brush teachers' hair.

'Sorry about that!' said Winnie.

At last everywhere was clean except for the Hall.

'Come on, Wilbur,' said Winnie, and she barged into the Hall with her mop and bucket and dusters and vacuum cleaner and sprays. The Hall was full of children sitting on the floor. They turned and smiled at Winnie. Winnie smiled back.

'Hello, little ordinaries!' said Winnie.

But the head teacher was standing in
front of the children, and he didn't smile.
He pointed at Winnie.

'OUT!' he said.

'But Mrs Parmar said . . .' began Winnie.

'OUT!' said the head teacher again. So
Winnie and Wilbur shuffled out of the Hall.

'Now how are we going to get the
cleaning done in time?' asked Winnie.

Wilbur shrugged.

'I know!' said Winnie. 'I'll do a spell to make myself invisible! Then I can clean and they won't see me. Where's my wand?'

They looked in the bucket of dirty water, in Winnie's pockets, under Winnie's hat.

'I've lost my wand! I've lost my magic!?' wailed Winnie.

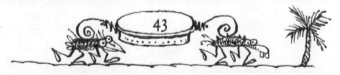

Then she had a thought. 'Ooo, I've remembered something from when I was little, Wilbur,' she said. 'I don't need magic to be invisible! I just need to cover my eyes with my hands. Come on, we'll go through the back door to the Hall so that the head teacher doesn't see the door opening. Hey, do you think they have arm and leg teachers as well as a head one, Wilbur?'

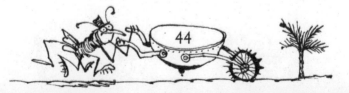

44

With a hand over her eyes, Winnie
lugged the vacuum cleaner and the
ladder and all the other bits into the Hall,
behind the head teacher. The children
laughed.

'Yes,' said the head teacher, not turning round. 'Yes, my story was rather amusing, wasn't it! Let me tell you another about the time I . . .' On he went with his boring story while the children laughed more and more. They cried. They held their tummies. There was even a puddle on the floor because they were laughing so much. On went the head teacher, but what the children were really laughing at was Winnie.

With a hand over her eyes, Winnie couldn't see anything. She tried to spray and polish the curtain, thinking it was a window.

'I'll have a go at those cobwebs next, Wilbur,' whispered Winnie.

She put the ladder up against the curtain and began to climb, still with one hand over her eyes. It was only Wilbur, holding with all his catty might, who stopped the ladder from crashing to the ground. Then Winnie bent over, and she showed her witchy bloomers.

'Yay!' cheered the children.

'What?' said Winnie, taking her hand from her face and realizing that she was balanced in the air. 'Oh, gnats' knickers! Don't let go, Wilbur! Ooooo! Noooo!'

CRASH! Wilbur wobbled, the ladder fell, and so did Winnie . . . right into the head teacher's arms.

'Hooray!' shouted the children, and they clapped and cheered.

The mess was terrible.

48

'Oh, where where where is my wand?'
wailed Winnie . . . and suddenly she
remembered. 'Your tail, Wilbur!'

Winnie grabbed the end of the sticky
plaster on Wilbur's tail and she pulled.

'YEEEEOOWWL!' yelled Wilbur,
clutching his tail that was now balder than
the head teacher's head.

But Winnie had her wand back and she
waved it around the room.

'Abracadabra!'

And instantly the place was tidy. The
glass glinted, the floor gleamed, and the
head teacher smiled.

'There!' said Winnie. 'All clean, and
you've got your voice back, Wilbur. It's
not every witch who can multi-task
like that, you know!'

51

WINNIE

and the
Ghost in the Post

'I want that!' said Winnie, pointing to the
telly. A smarmy vampire was lovingly
holding up a pen in the shape of a mini
broomstick.

'This pen can be yours!' said the
vampire. He seemed to be gazing straight
into Winnie's eyes.

'Can it really?' said Winnie. 'How's
that then?'

The vampire chuckled and winked.

'This pen is no ordinary pen. No! This pen doesn't need to be pushed over the paper. This pen will do the writing for you!'

'Ooo, that's wonderful!' said Winnie, clasping her hands together. 'Isn't it wonderful, Wilbur? Just what I need!'

Wilbur wasn't listening. He was busy writing a shopping list.

Eyes of newts

The vampire went on, 'This pen is the prize for our new poetry competition. Send in your poem and we'll choose which of you will win the pen.'

'Oo!' said Winnie, jumping up. 'Where's a pencil? Where's a bit of paper? I've got to get poetic, and you've got to help me, Wilbur!'

Wilbur glanced at Winnie's feet, then he wrote:

Polish for boots

Winnie waved her wand.

'Abracadabra!'

Instantly there appeared piles of paper and stacks of pens.

'I'm all ready!' she said. 'Now, what shall I put for my poem? I know! "The cat sat on the mat".'

Wilbur rolled his eyes.

A packet of tea

'But it's true,' said Winnie. 'Poetry should be about truth! You are a cat and you are sitting on a mat!'

Winnie tried to write down 'cat' and 'mat', but she couldn't even manage that.

56

'Oh, earwig belly buttons! You see,
that's why I need that pen! Pleeeease write
it for me, Wilbur!'

But Wilbur was still busy with his list.

Some fish for me

'Oh, my talents are wasted, that's what
they are!' Winnie tugged at her hair. 'If
only somebody would write down my
poem!'

Then Winnie had a thought. 'Oh, I know, I'll get one of those ghost writers!' she said. 'Where's that website for ghosts by post? Here it is!'

Winnie clicked the mouse to make the computer talk to her.

59

'PLEASE ANSWER THE FOLLOWING,' said the computer.

'KIND OF GHOST REQUIRED:

1) TO SCARE UNWANTED GUESTS

A) DRAGGING CLANKING CHAINS

B) HEADLESS

C) MOANING GREY WOMAN

2) TO ATTRACT VISITORS TO HISTORIC BUILDINGS

(A) , (B) , OR (C) , AS ABOVE.

3) TO DO SOME WRITING FOR YOU

A) THRILLERS

B) ROMANCES

C) POETRY'

'Definitely a 3(c),' said Winnie.
'Although I might try a 1(b) next time Auntie Aggie comes to stay!'

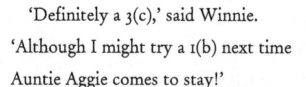

'SIZE OF GHOST WANTED

1) SMALL

2) MEDIUM

3) LARGE'

Winnie click-ticked (1). 'A small one can write as well as a big one, and it'll cost less.'

She got Wilbur to fill in the address.

SEND TO: Winnie the Witch, 13 Bat's Wing Crescent, Little Rats Bottom, LO1 3KP.

Winnie sent the form by witchmail,
which is fast. Next instant there was a
snap of the letter box and a slim envelope
fell onto the doormat.

'My ghost in the post!' said Winnie.

Wilbur sniffed the envelope, and hissed.
The envelope seemed to be breathing.

Winnie the Witch
13 Batswing Crescent
Little Rats Bottom
LO1 3KP

'Give it to me!' said Winnie. She tore
open the envelope, and tipped out . . .

'It looks like an old hanky!' said
Winnie, disappointed. 'Is it dead?' She
poked at the white thing. 'Oo, no it isn't!
Look, Wilbur!'

The flat white thing quivered. Then it rose elegantly into the air and bowed to Winnie and then to Wilbur.

'Good afternoooon!' it said. 'I am your poetic spooook. What do you desire me to doooooo?'

'Oh, dear little Post Ghost!' said Winnie. 'May I call you PG? I just want you to write a poem to win a competition.'

PG shuddered. 'Did you say "*just* write a poem"?'

'Er . . . yes,' said Winnie.

'My dear modom,' said PG in a quivering voice. 'There is no "just" about writing a poem.' PG put his ghostly hand to his ghostly brow. 'I have to be inspired before I can write!'

Winnie the Witch
is Babysitting again
little Ralfs k-tten
LOI SKF

65

'Have you?' said Winnie. 'How do we do that then?'

'Show me something beauooootiful,' said PG.

Winnie simpered and patted her hair.

PG pulled a face to show that he didn't think Winnie fitted the bill.

'What about Wilbur then?' said Winnie. 'Wilbur's beautiful. I'd like a poem about him.'

'I couldn't write about a smelly old cat!' PG looked around the room. 'Dear, oh dear. Nothing at all that I could uooooooooose. Is there, outside, perhaps, a lovely viewoooooo? Glistening with dewoooo? That would doooooo.'

'Ooo, I can hear the poem coming already!'
said Winnie, excited. 'Come outside, PG.'

It was a sunny day, but . . .

'I have it!' said PG. 'Hand me my quill.'
He began to write—

Oh, moooon, moooon

Beauooootiful moooon!

'You sound like a cow with belly ache!'
said Winnie.

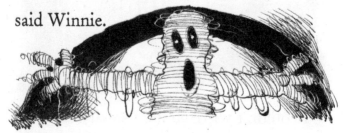

The little ghost flounced. *Sniff.* 'I *was*
going to go on with, "You look like a silver
spoooon". But I can't create when I'm upset.
I'm sensitive. I need ambiance and atmosphere
and appreciation to doooo my work . . .'

68

'Oh, I'm ever so sorry!' said Winnie.
'It's just that I haven't been to school and
I don't know much about poetry. I'll shut
up, shall I?'

So PG wrote about June (even though it
was April) and a balloon and a tune. And
Winnie tried very hard not to yawn.

Meanwhile, Wilbur was ready to go shopping.

'Ooo, wait, Wilbur!' called Winnie. 'I've got to put my poem in the post. And PG's got to be sent back toooo. And I do just need to go to the loooo before we go. Oh, heck, poetry seems to be catching!'

Winnie stuffed the poem into one envelope and the ghost into another.

'Quick! Let's get them posted!'

In the shop, Winnie and Wilbur looked
at their shopping list. It said—

Oh, moooon, moooon,

Beauoooootiful moooon!

'Oh, newts' nosedrops!' said Winnie.

'We've posted the wrong bit of paper!'

So Winnie and Wilbur went home
feeling cross. They slumped on sofas and
switched on the telly. There was the
vampire with the smile, just announcing . . .

'The winner of our pen competition is . . .
Winnie the Witch!'

'Oh! Oh! Oh!' Winnie was jumping up
and down as if she'd got ants in her pants.
'I won!'

The vampire read the winning poem:

'Eyes of newts

Polish for boots

A bag of tea

Some fish for me

Swede for the stew

A smell-fresh for the loo.'

'It's those "ooo" sounds that make this a truly poetic poem,' said the vampire. 'Well done, Winnie.'

Wilbur cleared his throat. He pointed a claw at himself.

'Oh, yes,' said Winnie. 'You wrote that, Wilbur. But will you still let me use the pen? Pretty please?'

The first thing Winnie used the pen-
that-writes-on-its-own for was to write a
poem for Wilbur.

The fat cat sat on the mat
He isn't a bat or even a rat
He is Wilbur, my cat
And I love him for that!

Mini
WINNIE

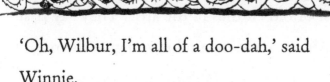

'Oh, Wilbur, I'm all of a doo-dah,' said
Winnie.

'Mrow?' asked Wilbur.

He was mashing worms, ready for tea.

'Wendy's coming round. I've ripped my
dress trying to reach for the best croakery
in the top cupboard. I've got nothing
smart to wear now, and you know what
Wendy's like!'

Winnie pulled all her pockets inside out to reveal a grey bit of slug gum and a couple of cross snails.

'I've not got any money, so I can't buy anything new. And, anyway, look at the clock! There's no time!' Winnie stroked her chin. 'Hmmn,' she said. 'But I have got a lot of old clothes in the attic. They say that fashions come around if you give them time. Come on, Wilbur! Let's see what we can find!'

Winnie pushed open the attic trapdoor and pulled down the attic ladder, and up she went. The attic was hot and dark and full of boxes and bags and suitcases. 'You use the torch, Wilbur, and I'll use the jar of glow-worms. See what you can find.'

78

Wilbur opened drawers and doors while
Winnie stuck her bottom in the air and
searched in bags and boxes. Soon there
were hats and hankies, bats and slippers,
books and flippers flying everywhere.

'Aha!' said Winnie, waving something.
'Mreow?'

'Oo, look, Wilbur! The shoes I wore on the day I fell in the duck pond! And the poncho I wore to that witches' disco. And see this? I bought it in a sale at Witch Wardrobe, but I've never worn it. That might do nicely, don't you think?' Winnie thrust a musty dusty fusty old skirt with labels still on it at Wilbur.

Wilbur stepped back.

'Meowatichoo!' he sneezed.

Winnie took a sniff.

''choo!' she went. She gave the skirt a shake and some purple and yellow moths flew out of it.

Wilbur was washing, licking a paw and then wiping the paw over his head.

'Heck, I need a wash too!' said Winnie, brushing cobwebs off her cardigan. Winnie licked her hand, then wiped it over her head, then licked it again.

'Yuck!' she said. 'I don't know what cat tastes like, Wilbur, but witch tastes disgusting!' She stuck out her tongue and licked the skirt. 'Euch! All hairy! It's like licking a Highland cow!'

Winnie bundled all the old clothes together. 'They can have a bath with me.'

Winnie ran a bath and tipped in frogspawn bubble bath. She threw in the clothes. Then she got in herself and sploshed around.

'Tra la la! Are you coming in too, Wilbur?'

'Mrrow!'

Winnie and Wilbur hung the clothes on the line, clipping them in place with baby alligators.

'Yeeow!' yelled Winnie. 'These pegs bite!'

Then they went inside for a snack of elephants' toenail crisps and eel slime tea.

'How long do clothes take to dry?' asked Winnie.

Wilbur shook his head and pointed out of the window.

'Oh, cockroach crusts!' said Winnie. 'It's raining!'

Winnie waved her wand angrily at the window.

'Abracadabra!'

Instantly the rain stopped. The grey clouds went. The sun came out and a gentle wind blew.

'Perfect for drying,' said Winnie.

But the wind began to blow harder. It blew so hard the birds couldn't cling to the trees. Winnie's knickers were in knots, her tights in a tangle, her dress in a mess, and her cardigan in a—

'Blooming heck!' said Winnie.

It blew so hard that the big man next door's washing came flying over.

'Cor, look at that!' said Winnie.

But Winnie's washing was escaping too. Wilbur ran outside and tried to catch the vests and socks, the bonnets and skirts.

'*Abracadabra!*' shouted Winnie, waving her wand. The wind stopped, but it was too late. Winnie's washing had fallen, splish-splosh, into muddy puddles.

'Oh, botherarmarations!' said Winnie. 'Put them all in the washing machine, Wilbur.'

Winnie filled the machine drawer with flea powder.

'Stand back!' said Winnie.

She pushed the button and . . .

kerpowowowowow! The machine coughed and collapsed. It spat out washing and springs and powder all over the place.

'Fleas' flippers! We'll have to do a proper witch wash. Quick!' said Winnie, looking at her watch. 'Where's the big cauldron?'

They put water and powder and the clothes into the cauldron. Wilbur found sticks and Winnie lit a fire. Then they both stirred the pot with old wands. Steam began to rise. The water began to bubble and boil.

'That'll get them clean,' said Winnie.

The clothes did get clean, but . . .

'They've shrunk!' wailed Winnie. 'I
won't fit in any of them! I'm too blooming
big! Pass my wand over, Wilbur.'

Winnie pointed the wand at herself.

Abracadabra! she shouted.

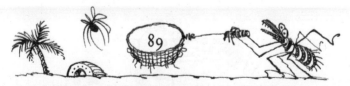

And in an instant there was empty
air where Winnie had been the moment
before. And there, on the floor, was a mini
Winnie, no bigger than a teaspoon with
scruffy hair.

'Ooer,' said mini Winnie. 'Aren't spiders BIG!
But at least I can wear the clothes now!'

Winnie tried on this . . . and that . . .
and those. 'This is the outfit, I think, Wilbur. Look
at the clock! I must make the tea.'

But mini Winnie couldn't reach the
work surface or the tap or the teapot. She
tried climbing up a chair leg. She tried
swinging up on the kettle flex.

'**Brrriiing!** Let me in!'

'It's the dooryell!' said mini Winnie. 'Wendy's
here! Quick! Where's that wand? *Abracadabra!*'

Instantly Winnie was back to normal size.
And standing in just her undies.

'Oh, double-heck!' she shrieked.

'**Brriiing brriiing!** Let me in!'

'What shall I do, Wilbur?' panicked Winnie.

Wilbur handed Winnie the patchwork
tea cosy.

'It's too small to cover me!' said Winnie.
'And, anyway, which bit of me goes through
which hole?'

But Wilbur was shaking his head and
pointing.

'Oh, I see!' said Winnie. 'Brillamaroodle
idea, Wilbur!'

Winnie quickly pointed her wand at the
pile of tiny clothes.

'*Abracadabra!*' she shouted, stirring
the clothes together into a sparkling whirl
that settled to reveal one new dress; a
patchwork dress that used all Winnie's
very favourite old clothes from all time.
'Oh, I love it!' said Winnie, slipping the
dress on. 'A perfect fit!'

93

'**Brrrriiiinggg!** Are you deaf, you silly witch?' yelled the dooryell.

'Coming!' said Winnie.

In came Wendy, bursting out of a tight brand-new outfit. 'Do you like it, Win?' she said. 'I bought it this morning from Frights. I suppose you're in your usual . . . oh!'

94

She stopped still. 'You're wearing something new! Where's it from?'

'From W & W,' said Winnie, doing a twirl. 'Do you like it?'

'Well, it is . . . um . . . unusual,' said Wendy. 'You know, there is something strangely familiar about it.'

'Never mind that,' said Winnie. 'Come and have some pond tea and toasted toadstools.'

And they all had tea together.

Enjoy more magic moments with
Winnie AND Wilbur